NEHEMIAH (BIBLICAL CHARACTER SERIES)

NEHEMIAH (BIBLICAL CHARACTER SERIES)

Bible Study Leader's Edition

JAMES G WHITELAW

Swackie Ltd

CONTENTS

Introduction		1
1	Are we ready for Revival?	2
2	Ask for revival	8
3	Plan for revival	13
4	Rebuilding the walls	18
5	Opposition to rebuilding	23
6	Helping the needy	28
7	Psychological Opposition	34
8	Taking Stock	39
9	Instruction	45
10	Confession	49
11	Rededication	55
12	Restoration	60
13	Dedication	64
14	Reform	70

15 Conclusion	75
Author's Note	76

Introduction

Nehemiah is a fascinating book which relates the revival in Israel under Nehemiah around 500 BC. Nehemiah relates the entire period so well, that it is a classic blueprint for any and every revival since, especially revivals in the Church.

This book plots Nehemiah's progress and shows how it relates to us to today and what we should expect in our next revival. Indeed, the book goes further and details the steps we must take to ensure revival in the Church.

The book searches for a Nehemiah in our time, a man who will lead our Church and our nation to true revival. It asks some very difficult and searching questions and shows why a determined effort and dedication will be required before revival visits us again.

The book concludes by exhorting our reader to '**Be that man**'

Jim Whitelaw is a committed Christian and an author. Jim was brought up in a Christian home from the day he was born but has not always found the road easy or straightforward. This gives him an insight into the difficulties the characters in the Bible must have faced, in his Biblical Character Series, and helps him to look at many of the failures in a different and forgiving light.

Jim Whitelaw is semi-retired after a life largely spent at sea. He is a grandfather with 5 grandchildren and lives in the northeast of Scotland. He writes mostly what is on his heart and interests him, so has more than one niche.

BSLE: All comments and help only in the BSLE are shown like this. These comments and hints should be used as a pause to discuss the matters shown.

CHAPTER 1

Are we ready for Revival?

Nehemiah Chapter 1
The words of Nehemiah son of Hakaliah:
In the month of Kislev in the twentieth year, while I was in the citadel of Susa, Hanani, one of my brothers, came from Judah with some other men, and I questioned them about the Jewish remnant that had survived the exile, and also about Jerusalem.
They said to me, "Those who survived the exile and are back in the province are in great trouble and disgrace. The wall of Jerusalem is broken down, and its gates have been burned with fire."
When I heard these things, I sat down and wept. For some days I mourned and fasted and prayed before the God of heaven. Then I said:
"Lord, the God of heaven, the great and awesome God, who keeps his covenant of love with those who love him and keep his commandments, let your ear be attentive and your eyes open to hear the prayer your servant is praying before you day and night for your servants, the people of Israel. I confess the sins we Israelites, including myself and my father's family, have committed against you. We have acted very wickedly toward

you. We have not obeyed the commands, decrees and laws you gave your servant Moses.

"Remember the instruction you gave your servant Moses, saying, 'If you are unfaithful, I will scatter you among the nations, but if you return to me and obey my commands, then even if your exiled people are at the farthest horizon, I will gather them from there and bring them to the place I have chosen as a dwelling for my Name.'

"They are your servants and your people, whom you redeemed by your great strength and your mighty hand. Lord, let your ear be attentive to the prayer of this your servant and to the prayer of your servants who delight in revering your name. Give your servant success today by granting him favor in the presence of this man."

I was cupbearer to the king.

For days, Nehemiah wept, fasted and prayed after he received word about the condition of Jerusalem. The news that Jerusalem was in a terrible state and the people suffering cut him to the bone. He tells God that he has been praying night and day.

How long did Nehemiah weep and pray? It's not very clear, but he tells us that the messenger came in Chislev, which would have been around November, December. The following chapter tells us that he was in the King's presence in the month of Nisan, which is around March or April. That's a difference of four months.

We do not know how long these days were, we are only told some days, but we know that the man who was broken before God came out of this period alone with God, with great purpose and a plan of action.

BSLE: Are we broken when we consider the state of our Church or our country?

Look around your town or city. Walk down the streets, go to a football match or a large gathering, look at the crowds. What do you see? Do you see happy people just going about their business, or do you see millions of lost souls destined for hell?

Go to any Church in your area. How many empty pews do you see? Benches that used to be crammed, families squeezed in tight together. Look at the old Church buildings now turned into dance halls, nightclubs, bingo halls, houses. Does this not cut you to the bone, just as the tale of Jerusalem did to Nehemiah?

Nehemiah was one man. Only one man was concerned about Jerusalem. Only one man was disturbed enough to mourn and fast and pray before God. But, one man was all that God needed.

BSLE: God only needs one man. Who will be that man?

Only the first four verses of this book relate to the agony of Nehemiah, but these four verses are vital to understanding the entire book. They are crucial to understanding the great passion which drove Nehemiah to achieve great works.

Let us consider this man carefully, as we live in a similar time. We don't need to wait for a messenger. We can see it all with our own eyes and read about it on our computer screens. We do not need a messenger to tell us that the walls of our Churches have been broken down and the gates burned with fire.

We do not need a messenger to inform us that our Church today is in great trouble and disgrace. It came as a great shock to Nehemiah, but we have got used to it gradually and been lulled into accepting it as the new normal.

It is not normal. It is not acceptable. We need to stop and think about what the Churches in our land are today. When we do that, if it doesn't cut us to the bone, then there is something far wrong with us as Christians.

BSLE: Stop and think about your area, your Church, your country. How does that make you feel?

It needs to affect us in the same way the news of Jerusalem affected Nehemiah. We should be mourning, weeping and crying out to God. Jerusalem is God's holy city, the centre of the entire world, the hope of every nation. The Church today is God's people, the centre of his plans and the only hope the whole world has.

We need to mourn when we realise that the Church is in complete disarray and total disgrace. Further, without a functioning Church, the world will continue to descend into darkness, and millions of lost souls will continue along the road to hell. Little wonder that Nehemiah wept.

BSLE: Are we mourning? Are we crying out to God?

Where are our tears? Where is our fasting? Where is our mourning? Where is our Nehemiah today?

Is it our God-given right to Revival? Is it our right to claim God's promise of revival in scripture? No, it is not unless we hold up our end of the bargain. Notice, Nehemiah didn't start by asking God for anything at all. Instead, he began in the proper place, admitting responsibility for his dire position.

Nehemiah wasn't born when Jerusalem fell. Nehemiah wasn't around when the nation ran after every false God on the planet. So how could it possibly have anything to do with Nehemiah? How could Nehemiah possibly be to blame for any of the past troubles?

We seriously need to learn about collective responsibility. We all tend to hide behind the excuse, 'It's other Curches. We have remained true. We're not so bad as some other Churches'. Sorry, that is simply pride talking. Your Church is empty, just the same as the other Churches.

BSLE: How has our Church declined over the past fifty years?

We need to get on our knees before God just as Nehemiah did and start by confessing our sins. We need to admit how we have failed God. We need to acknowledge how we have put worldly things before him. We need to confess how we are sitting comfortably in our homes while the Church of Jesus is in ruins around us.

We need to be broken by God so that he can use us for his great work. God cannot use any of us while one single vestige of personal pride remains within us. God cannot use people who are like the Pharisees.

These are not comfortable things to say, mainly as they apply to me, just as much, if not more than anyone else. But, being comfortable is not going to solve the problem. Being comfortable is not going to bring on revival. Being comfortable is not going to restore the Church to its former glory. Only a contrite and humble heart is going to do that.

Remember the promise back in 2 Chronicles chapter 7 v 14? 'If my people, who are called by my name, will humble themselves and pray and seek my face and turn from their wicked ways, then I will hear from heaven, and I will forgive their sin and will heal their land.'

We have heard this verse quite a lot, have probably heard many sermons on it and have heard it used to call upon God in prayer for revival. Yet, we haven't had a revival.

You see, our problem is the very first requirement in that verse. It is challenging for us to humble ourselves. We have prayed. We have sought his face. So why have we had no answer? God is faithful. If he says he will do something, he will do it.

If God says he will hear from heaven, forgive us and heal our land, he will do it. If he is not doing it, it is not because he is deaf, a liar, or unable to do it. It's because we have not carried out our bit.

BSLE: Have we called on the name of the Lord for Revival? Have we sought his face? Did we firstly, really humble ourselves?

Nehemiah humbled himself before all, even before the mightiest ruler in the world at that time. He took his life in his hands, being in the King's presence, looking sad, and then to have the audacity to request the King's help in restoring Jerusalem. Why would the King care about Jerusalem, just another city in his empire?

He could well have turned around and, given Nehemiah's audacity, had him put to death, and Nehemiah knew this. Yet, the concern for Jerusalem drove him forward into this challenging situation, with only a prayer to his God to support him.

What is going to drive us forward? What is firstly going to drive us to our knees? What is going to take us to the point where we will give up everything we have for the opportunity to gain revival in our land? How badly do we want revival?

BSLE: Are we really willing to give up every single thing in our lives for revival?

We are not going to see revival until we have a man like Nehemiah. We only need one man. Nehemiah was one man, the only one concerned enough about Jerusalem. When we have one man like Nehemiah, we will see revival throughout our land.

Is that man, or woman, listening today? Is there someone listening to this message here today who is willing to place their entire life on hold in the pursuit of revival? That is what it will take.

God is faithful; we have proved that over and over. If we carry out his requirements, he will be faithful and do what he said. If we humble ourselves before him, he will heal our land. Brothers and Sisters, what is it going to take before we will humble ourselves before God and confess our sins and the sins of our fathers in the Church.

Our Churches are in ruins, and our land is in utter chaos, yet we cling to our comfortable lifestyle, ambling along to Church a few times a week. Still, the majority of our time is spent at ease, enjoying a laid-back pleasant, relaxing lifestyle.

How far should our Churches fall before we fall on our faces before God and commit every fibre of our bodies to his cause?

BSLE: Discuss the entire chapter and pray about what you have discussed. Encourage group to read next chapter before meeting again.

CHAPTER 2

Ask for revival

Nehemiah Chapter 2 V 1-10

In the month of Nisan in the twentieth year of King Artaxerxes, when wine was brought for him, I took the wine and gave it to the king. I had not been sad in his presence before, so the king asked me, "Why does your face look so sad when you are not ill? This can be nothing but sadness of heart."

I was very much afraid, but I said to the king, "May the king live forever! Why should my face not look sad when the city where my ancestors are buried lies in ruins, and its gates have been destroyed by fire?"

The king said to me, "What is it you want?"

Then I prayed to the God of heaven, and I answered the king, "If it pleases the king and if your servant has found favor in his sight, let him send me to the city in Judah where my ancestors are buried so that I can rebuild it."

Then the king, with the queen sitting beside him, asked me, "How long will your journey take, and when will you get back?" It pleased the king to send me; so I set a time.

I also said to him, "If it pleases the king, may I have letters to the governors of Trans-Euphrates, so that they will provide me safe-conduct until I arrive in Judah? And may I have a letter to Asaph, keeper of the royal park, so he will give me timber to make beams for the gates of the citadel by the temple and for the city wall and for the residence I will occupy?" And because the gracious hand of my God was on me, the king granted my requests. So I went to the governors of Trans-Euphrates and gave them the king's letters. The king had also sent army officers and cavalry with me.

When Sanballat the Horonite and Tobiah the Ammonite official heard about this, they were very much disturbed that someone had come to promote the welfare of the Israelites.

How often do we pray to God for revival when we have not completed the first step beforehand? In the last chapter, we saw what was necessary to make us ready for revival. Once we have done that, it is the right time to start asking for it.

This first step is critical. It is so important that I want to stress that if we have not successfully concluded the first step, there is little point in progressing to the second step, asking for revival. So if we have not completed the first step, go back and go over chapter one until you get it right, regardless of how long it takes.

BSLE: Have we taken lesson one onboard? Are we ready for revival?

We are always in a hurry, and we live in an age where we expect everything instantly. We read through the first step and then move quickly to the next step without digesting or putting the first step into practice. How many men do we know who gets a home assembly piece of furniture, pulls everything out of the box and starts putting it together without even looking at the instructions?

The book of Nehemiah is like that, and if you do not read all the instructions and put them into practice, exactly as shown, then it will all go wrong. Further down the line, when making your furniture up, you inevitably come upon a piece that should have been put in earlier but can't go in now because some other part is blocking it.

If you don't ensure that you are ready for revival, you will move on to the request stage and find yourself blocked. How many times have we prayed for revival in our Churches, but we still do not have it? The simple truth is that you cannot get revival until you are ready for revival

It just will not work, and you have to go right back to the beginning and start again. Only when we are ready can we move on to the next step, asking for revival.

BSLE: Are we ready for revival?

There was only one person who could have granted Nehemiah's request, the King. It is the same for us. The only person who can grant our request is the King of kings, our father in heaven. You cannot pray to any saint or even to the mother of Jesus. These were fallible people just like us.

Jesus has opened the way for us to boldly enter the throne room of heaven. When he died for us, the veil of the temple was torn in two, which symbolised the barrier between God and us had been torn down, and we could now bring our requests to God through the advocacy of Jesus.

If we are ready for revival, then we will already be found at the throne of God. We will already have had long periods alone with him where we have been broken, wept and mourned for our Church and our land. We will have personally arrived at the position where nothing else in this world matters a jot to us, save the restoration of God's Church and the healing of our land.

This passage only relates to the final request to God, which is public and open for all to see. In truth, Nehemiah did not need the approval of the emperor. He already had the support of the King of kings. This was simply a display of intent and a formalising of the plan which God had set Nehemiah's heart.

Christians often get the name of being sad or melancholy. But, unfortunately, the world thinks we should always be happy and ask the same question the King asked Nehemiah, 'Why are you sad?'

There are times to be happy, and there are also times to be sad. When we read a joyous passage in scripture, which we will do later in this study, it is right to be happy and overjoyed, but right now, reading this passage, it is certainly not a happy message and not a time to be happy.

It is also little wonder that many Christians look constantly sad, given the state of the Church at the moment. Christians are right to be concerned and even in grief, as Nehemiah was, and remain in this state until the Church's position changes.

BSLE: Are we sad for our Church and for our nation?

We have one significant advantage over Nehemiah in that we do not have to come to our King in fear. Instead, we can come to an awesome God, knowing that He delights in our requests and that he delights in granting our requests. He also wants us to come boldly before him and make bold requests, just as Nehemiah did.

When we come before the King of kings, we must pour out our hearts to him and specifically request everything we need to build his Church so that it will glorify him. We must be sure that our desire is for his glory and not our own, as all our efforts will fail if this is the case.

We need to be specific and tell God about any problems we see arising and the result we wish to help us in his work. Then, like Nehemiah, we will most likely find that we will be granted much more than we requested, and we will have royal protection around us as we go about his business.

BSLE: What do we need from God for revival to break out?

However, having protection does not mean that we will not have opposition. Satan is happy with the Church ineffective, and like Sanballat and Tobiah, he will be sorely displeased by anyone seeking the Church's welfare.

Are you ready for revival? Has God broken you and remoulded you into a new creation? Is your single desire in life to see God's Church rebuilt and glorifying his name?

Is there nothing else in your life as important as God's Church? Are you sick in your heart by what you see as you examine the Church in our land and your local area? In the private of your own home, do you weep before God for the church?

I'm still looking for a Nehemiah, and this is what he will resemble. Our Nehemiah will be a man or a woman who has been broken by God, broken by grief for the Church and remoulded anew by long periods alone with God.

He will emerge from God's presence with a single-mindedness and a passion that will let nothing stand in his way. His passion and devotion will drive him forward when the way seems blocked. His compelling desire for revival will press him onward when all seem against him.

Our Nehemiah will come from the throne of grace with great purpose and with a plan of action. But, first, he will make it known what he seeks to do and publicly make his request to God for his help.

Where is our Nehemiah today? Where are our tears? Where is our grief for a Church lying in ruins around us?

BSLE: Discuss the entire chapter and pray about what you have discussed. Encourage group to read next chapter before meeting again.

CHAPTER 3

Plan for revival

<u>Nehemiah Chapter 2 v 11-20</u>

I went to Jerusalem, and after staying there three days I set out during the night with a few others. I had not told anyone what my God had put in my heart to do for Jerusalem. There were no mounts with me except the one I was riding on.

By night I went out through the Valley Gate toward the Jackal Well and the Dung Gate, examining the walls of Jerusalem, which had been broken down, and its gates, which had been destroyed by fire. Then I moved on toward the Fountain Gate and the King's Pool, but there was not enough room for my mount to get through; so I went up the valley by night, examining the wall. Finally, I turned back and reentered through the Valley Gate. The officials did not know where I had gone or what I was doing, because as yet I had said nothing to the Jews or the priests or nobles or officials or any others who would be doing the work.

Then I said to them, "You see the trouble we are in: Jerusalem lies in ruins, and its gates have been burned with fire. Come, let us rebuild the wall of Jerusalem, and we will no longer be in disgrace." I also told them about the gracious hand of my God on me and what the king had said to me.

They replied, "Let us start rebuilding." So they began this good work.

But when Sanballat the Horonite, Tobiah the Ammonite official and Geshem the Arab heard about it, they mocked and ridiculed us. "What is this you are doing?" they asked. "Are you rebelling against the king?"

I answered them by saying, "The God of heaven will give us success. We his servants will start rebuilding, but as for you, you have no share in Jerusalem or any claim or historic right to it."

We have examined being ready for revival, and in the last chapter, we looked at asking for revival, and now we need to step out in faith and plan for revival. If your previous steps are not in place, you will feel deeply uncomfortable here, but if you are ready to prepare for revival, you will know, as God will already have answered your prayers with the resources required to begin your task.

The next step is to take stock of the situation, figure out what is needed, and start making a plan. Where do you start looking? You start looking at the point where you must start working, and that is on the walls. Nehemiah knew that for security, he needed to fix the walls. A remnant had returned earlier and had carried out some work, but it was all at risk if the walls are broken down.

In the Christian Church today, and it's the same before every movement of God, the walls of the Church are broken down. The walls represent the Church's doctrine, and we will find that our doctrine has been compromised and broken, allowing all sorts of activities to occur which are not in line with what God has instructed in his word.

BSLE: Are the walls of our Churches broken down? Have we allowed our doctrine to slip? In which ways have we compromised?

You may find that there are ecumenical relations with religions that do not conform to Biblical standards. These could be Islam, Mormons, Jehovah Witnesses and even Catholics.

Some may take offence adding Catholics to this list, and indeed Catholics have some excellent points, some great people, but the bottom line is they do not conform to Scripture as written in the Bible on many issues.

The Catholic Church believe the Pope is infallible when the Bible tells us there is none good save Jesus, who lived a perfect life. The Catholics also pray to saints who are dead. The Bible is clear-cut that supplication can only be made to God through the person of Jesus, who is our advocate at the right-hand side of God. These are only a few things, but the Catholic Church has many false doctrines.

Where our doctrine and standards have slipped, this is what we must examine and document. These must be restored and put right before we can progress. The process of documentation and examination of the condition of the walls should be kept private as many will cause problems if they know what you are doing. Unfortunately, many with a vested interest in the status quo will do anything to stop change.

BSLE: Are there those within the Church who do not want change?

We must take as long as required to carry out this task and do a thorough job so that nothing manages to escape us and leave a weak point in the Church later. Only once we are satisfied that we have documented all the weak and broken areas we publicise our immediate plan.

Note in verse twelve, Nehemiah said that God put it in his mind to do these things. We can never achieve anything of ourselves. Only that which is born of God will succeed.

At this point, we must consult with those involved with the Church and advise them of our plans. However, we should be careful as not all will welcome them, and they will have no issue involving those from outside the Church in their attempts to stop the rebuilding work.

Just as Nehemiah told Sanballat, Tobiah and Geshem, we must be firm that these people have no part in the Church, and we must be strong in our belief that God's plans will prevail against all the wiles of the devil.

BSLE: How will we counter the opposition which will surely come?

Apart from the walls, Nehemiah was also intent on repairing the gates. The gates control who come and go and who can interact with our citizens. In our Churches today, there is an open season on who can join, and once they are in, they try to corrupt other believers with false and misleading doctrines.

We must also take stock and document the condition of our gates to the Church and see what repairs must be made. We must guard the pulpits and teaching of our Churches to ensure that no one enters who would propagate false beliefs.

Sadly today, Churches are so far away from the truth of God that deacons and elders are in place who do not know God. Even our pulpits are filled with enemies of Christ. The Church's gates have been burned with fire, and there is nothing to stop Satan from walking right in whenever he wishes.

BSLE: Are all your Church leaders and officers born again Christians who will welcome revival?

Because the gates are broken down, these false teachers have also destroyed the walls from within. They have pulled the stones from our walls, one by one. They have replaced sound Biblical doctrine with a doctrine from hell.

They have replaced purity with promiscuousness. They have replaced Christianity with carnality. They have replaced Love with lust. They have replaced Grace with greed. They have replaced Faith with fallacy, and they have replaced hope with hopelessness.

True Christians looking at the Church must grieve when they see the condition of her walls and gates, and our first task must be to answer the call of our Nehemiah when he comes to rebuild our walls and replace the gates.

When the call comes from our Nehemiah, he points out our dangerous position and shows our Churches are desolate. Therefore, as the people of God, we need to be ready to reply, like the inhabitants of Jerusalem, 'We will arise and build that we may no longer be a reproach'.

BSLE: Discuss the entire chapter and pray about what you have discussed. Encourage group to read next chapter before meeting again.

CHAPTER 4

Rebuilding the walls

Nehemiah Chapter 3
Eliashib the high priest and his fellow priests went to work and rebuilt the Sheep Gate. They dedicated it and set its doors in place, building as far as the Tower of the Hundred, which they dedicated, and as far as the Tower of Hananel. The men of Jericho built the adjoining section, and Zakkur son of Imri built next to them.

The Fish Gate was rebuilt by the sons of Hassenaah. They laid its beams and put its doors and bolts and bars in place. Meremoth son of Uriah, the son of Hakkoz, repaired the next section. Next to him Meshullam son of Berekiah, the son of Meshezabel, made repairs, and next to him Zadok son of Baana also made repairs. The next section was repaired by the men of Tekoa, but their nobles would not put their shoulders to the work under their supervisors.

The Jeshanah Gate was repaired by Joiada son of Paseah and Meshullam son of Besodeiah. They laid its beams and put its doors with their bolts and bars in place. Next to them, repairs were made by men from Gibeon and Mizpah—Melatiah of Gibeon and Jadon of Meronoth—places under the authority of the governor of Trans-Euphrates. Uzziel son of Harhaiah, one of the goldsmiths, repaired the next section; and Hananiah, one of the perfume-makers, made repairs next to that. They restored Jerusalem as far as the Broad Wall. Rephaiah son of Hur, ruler of a half-district of Jerusalem, repaired the next section. Adjoining this, Jedaiah son of Harumaph made repairs opposite his house, and Hattush son of Hashabneiah made repairs next to him. Malkijah son of Harim and Hasshub son of Pahath-Moab repaired another section and the Tower of the Ovens. Shallum son of Hallohesh, ruler of a half-district of Jerusalem, repaired the next section with the help of his daughters.

The Valley Gate was repaired by Hanun and the residents of Zanoah. They rebuilt it and put its doors with their bolts and bars in place. They also repaired a thousand cubits of the wall as far as the Dung Gate.

The Dung Gate was repaired by Malkijah son of Rekab, ruler of the district of Beth Hakkerem. He rebuilt it and put its doors with their bolts and bars in place.

The Fountain Gate was repaired by Shallun son of Kol-Hozeh, ruler of the district of Mizpah. He rebuilt it, roofing it over and putting its doors and bolts and bars in place. He also repaired the wall of the Pool of Siloam, by the King's Garden, as far as the steps going down from the City of David. Beyond him, Nehemiah son of Azbuk, ruler of a half-district of Beth Zur, made repairs up to a point opposite the tombs of David, as far as the artificial pool and the House of the Heroes.

Next to him, the repairs were made by the Levites under Rehum son of Bani. Beside him, Hashabiah, ruler of half the district of Keilah, carried out repairs for his district. Next to him, the repairs were made by their fellow Levites under Binnui son of Henadad, ruler of the other half-district of Keilah. Next to him, Ezer son of Jeshua, ruler of Mizpah, repaired another section, from a point facing the ascent to the armory as far as the angle of the wall. Next to him, Baruch son of Zabbai zealously repaired another section, from the angle to the entrance of the house of Eliashib the high priest. Next to him, Meremoth son of Uriah, the son of

Hakkoz, repaired another section, from the entrance of Eliashib's house to the end of it.

The repairs next to him were made by the priests from the surrounding region. Beyond them, Benjamin and Hasshub made repairs in front of their house; and next to them, Azariah son of Maaseiah, the son of Ananiah, made repairs beside his house. Next to him, Binnui son of Henadad repaired another section, from Azariah's house to the angle and the corner, and Palal son of Uzai worked opposite the angle and the tower projecting from the upper palace near the court of the guard. Next to him, Pedaiah son of Parosh and the temple servants living on the hill of Ophel made repairs up to a point opposite the Water Gate toward the east and the projecting tower. Next to them, the men of Tekoa repaired another section, from the great projecting tower to the wall of Ophel.

Above the Horse Gate, the priests made repairs, each in front of his own house. Next to them, Zadok son of Immer made repairs opposite his house. Next to him, Shemaiah son of Shekaniah, the guard at the East Gate, made repairs. Next to him, Hananiah son of Shelemiah, and Hanun, the sixth son of Zalaph, repaired another section. Next to them, Meshullam son of Berekiah made repairs opposite his living quarters. Next to him, Malkijah, one of the goldsmiths, made repairs as far as the house of the temple servants and the merchants, opposite the Inspection Gate, and as far as the room above the corner; and between the room above the corner and the Sheep Gate the goldsmiths and merchants made repairs.

You may remember, away back in chapter one, I asked, 'Where are our tears? Where is our fasting? Where is our mourning? Where is our Nehemiah today?'

The reason I am looking for our Nehemiah is this chapter. This is what happens when we have a Nehemiah. The energy, passion and drive which Nehemiah has, extends to all he comes into contact with, and all the people set themselves to the task which Nehemiah has determined.

Not everyone will participate at the same level. The Tekoit nobles did not support the work, but Baruch, the son of Zabbai worked zealously, we are told. It will be the same in the Church. There will be those who throw their all into it and those who hold back.

Some will be like Benjamin and Hasshub, who only repaired the area in their vicinity, while others may be like Shallum, who even got his daughters involved in the rebuilding.

BSLE: When we begin rebuilding the Church, how involved will you be?

The whole population of God's people will be mobilized and energized to work. Nehemiah ensures that the entire circle of the walls are under repair and that no part is left out. At the same time, he ensures all the gates are replaced and secured.

It is a time of great work, extreme busyness. The vast majority of the people are single-minded on the job at hand. Without Nehemiah, none of this would have happened, but it is now plain to see what one energizing source can accomplish when it comes with the backing of God almighty.

Please take note that the first to put their hands to the work were the priests. They consecrated the gates and hung the doors. It needs to be the same in the Church. The Church leaders need to be the first to go to work, and they need to work on the gates. In plain language, they need to protect who enters into our pulpits. This is the very first step.

As we read on through the list, it takes us on a complete circuit of the city, starting at the sheep gate and coming round back to where they started. All manner of people were involved. It wasn't just left to masons and bricklayers to do the work. Everybody was involved.

The text mentions goldsmith, perfumers, officials, daughters, Levites, Temple servants, gatekeepers and merchants. All these were involved in the work and many more who we are not told what their occupation was. Everybody was involved in the effort of rebuilding the walls.

BSLE: What is our responsibility for the condition the Church is in? Is it our responsibility to fix it?

The truth is everyone is responsible for the condition of the walls, so it needs every one of us to be involved in their repair. The time for repentance and remorse has passed, and everyone must set to work rebuilding the walls, regardless of their past sins and failings.

Like Jerusalem, most in the Church have failed in the past and stood idle while the City of God is in ruins. That is in the past and must be forgotten as all strive towards securing the Church. There will be consecration on the journey and during the work, but the job will be great, and it will be a considerable effort to complete.

BSLE: Discuss the entire chapter and pray about what you have discussed. Encourage group to read next chapter before meeting again.

CHAPTER 5

Opposition to rebuilding

<u>Nehemiah Chapter 4</u>

When Sanballat heard that we were rebuilding the wall, he became angry and was greatly incensed. He ridiculed the Jews, and in the presence of his associates and the army of Samaria, he said, "What are those feeble Jews doing? Will they restore their wall? Will they offer sacrifices? Will they finish in a day? Can they bring the stones back to life from those heaps of rubble—burned as they are?"

Tobiah the Ammonite, who was at his side, said, "What they are building—even a fox climbing up on it would break down their wall of stones!"

Hear us, our God, for we are despised. Turn their insults back on their own heads. Give them over as plunder in a land of captivity. Do not cover up their guilt or blot out their sins from your sight, for they have thrown insults in the face of the builders.

So we rebuilt the wall till all of it reached half its height, for the people worked with all their heart.

But when Sanballat, Tobiah, the Arabs, the Ammonites and the people of Ashdod heard that the repairs to Jerusalem's walls had gone ahead and that the gaps were being closed, they were very angry. They all plotted together to come and fight against Jerusalem and stir up trouble against it. But we prayed to our God and posted a guard day and night to meet this threat.

Meanwhile, the people in Judah said, "The strength of the laborers is giving out, and there is so much rubble that we cannot rebuild the wall."

Also our enemies said, "Before they know it or see us, we will be right there among them and will kill them and put an end to the work."

Then the Jews who lived near them came and told us ten times over, "Wherever you turn, they will attack us."

Therefore I stationed some of the people behind the lowest points of the wall at the exposed places, posting them by families, with their swords, spears and bows. After I looked things over, I stood up and said to the nobles, the officials and the rest of the people, "Don't be afraid of them. Remember the Lord, who is great and awesome, and fight for your families, your sons and your daughters, your wives and your homes."

When our enemies heard that we were aware of their plot and that God had frustrated it, we all returned to the wall, each to our own work.

From that day on, half of my men did the work, while the other half were equipped with spears, shields, bows and armor. The officers posted themselves behind all the people of Judah who were building the wall. Those who carried materials did their work with one hand and held a weapon in the other, and each of the builders wore his sword at his side as he worked. But the man who sounded the trumpet stayed with me.

Then I said to the nobles, the officials and the rest of the people, "The work is extensive and spread out, and we are widely separated from each other along the wall. Wherever you hear the sound of the trumpet, join us there. Our God will fight for us!"

So we continued the work with half the men holding spears, from the first light of dawn till the stars came out. At that time I also said to the people, "Have every man and his helper stay inside Jerusalem at night, so they can serve us as guards by night and as workers by day." Neither I nor my brothers nor my men nor the guards with me took off our clothes; each had his weapon, even when he went for water.

We do not see much opposition from Satan these days. The truth is we are not causing him many problems. We are not stealing many souls from him. On the contrary, we are pretty much allowing him free reign in changing the basis of society and even changing how Churches operate.

However, if we start causing him problems, you can be sure he will react. For example, if we have a Nehemiah who intends to rebuild the Church's walls, he will be outraged and attack us in any way he can. This is not something which we can avoid, so we must prepare for it.

BSLE: In what areas will the world be unhappy when we start changing and affirming our beliefs?

The opposition will start with ridicule and mockery, but the Church will continue on its path, rebuilding the walls and replacing the gates. However, as the work progresses, just like the Jews here, we will get weary. It's not just a weariness of work, but trying to work while keeping an eye open for attack, keeping your sword by you all the time, not being even able to relax at night.

What we will discover in this period, as we start rebuilding, is that Satan is real. He is alive and still going around like a roaring lion. Everything we do will be ridiculed, questioned, disputed, undermined, stalled and opposed. If there is one thing Satan does not want, it is for the Church's walls to be rebuilt.

BSLE: Do we see much opposition in our Church at the moment?

Over the years in which the Church has declined, Satan has opened channels into the Church in many ways. He has those outside who mock and rage, but he also has those inside who quietly spread false ideas and sap the Church's strength. He can do this because the gates are broken, and his people can walk in at will.

When we try to change this, rebuild the walls and put up the gates again, he will not take it lying down. His whole fury will be released on us, and without our God at our side, we would not stand.

But praise God, he is on our side. It is his work we do, and he will make sure we succeed. Like Nehemiah, we need to turn to him at even the first sign of trouble and ask for help. These are spiritual battles, and we will not succeed in our own strength.

While we rely on God for protection, that does not mean we take it easy. Note, the builders had their weapons by their hands at all times. They could not venture anywhere without their weapons in their hands and did not even take off their clothes at night. This is because they had to be ready to fight at all times.

BSLE: What is our best weapon of defence? Do we know how to use it?

We also must prepare and always have our weapons at hand. Our weapon is the best there is, the two-edged sword of God's word. We must always have it with us and know how to use it. We must be familiar with it and be ready to deploy it at any time.

We are not going on a Sunday school picnic. We are going into battle, which will determine whether we can complete rebuilding the Church's walls and the beginning of a revival in our land.

Just as in this passage, the work is extensive, and it will be tiresome work. Some will be out doing the rebuilding, but others will be deployed in defence. Some will be rebuilding the Church's walls against fierce opposition in the Church, but there will also be those who may appear not to be doing anything but are deployed in defence, our prayer warriors.

None will be idle. All will be working furiously on the work at hand. It may be that some will be preaching, teaching, fighting court battles, disputing and debating, going into schools, universities, government and all manner of places, fighting the corner for the Church. All of these will depend on the warriors deployed to support and protect them by prayer.

BSLE: How is prayer within our Church? Are there many who participate in the weekly prayer meeting? Do you have a weekly prayer meeting?

Of course, let us not forget those who came in when the gates were broken down. There will also be those who will seek to stall, derail, subvert, hamper and stop the work. There will be those within who will aid our enemies. But, let us remind them, it is not us who is doing this work. It is God himself, and let us further remind them the words of Jesus, 'I will build my Church and the gates of hell will not prevail against it.'

We will overcome and frustrate the enemy just as God's people did in this passage. We will thwart their efforts by consistent alertness and dedication to the work. We will work by day and guard by night.

Our enemies will plan an outright attack on us, but our God will inform us of their plans and frustrate them. For all that they try, the work will progress, and the walls will be built.

When our enemies see the progress of our work, they will become even angrier, and we will have to take measures to protect the Church. Attacks could come in many ways, and at many places, we must be ready to listen for the call from our leaders to rally to any point where the enemy attacks. Therefore, while we work, we must also always be ready to fight.

We are on the winning side. The progress we have made will strengthen our hands, and we will persevere in rebuilding the church. Yet, fear may come upon some, and we must support each other and remind each other that we are more than conquerors through Christ Jesus.

BSLE: Discuss the entire chapter and pray about what you have discussed. Encourage group to read next chapter before meeting again.

CHAPTER 6

Helping the needy

Nehemiah Chapter 5

Now the men and their wives raised a great outcry against their fellow Jews. Some were saying, "We and our sons and daughters are numerous; in order for us to eat and stay alive, we must get grain."

Others were saying, "We are mortgaging our fields, our vineyards and our homes to get grain during the famine."

Still others were saying, "We have had to borrow money to pay the king's tax on our fields and vineyards. Although we are of the same flesh and blood as our fellow Jews and though our children are as good as theirs, yet we have to subject our sons and daughters to slavery. Some of our daughters have already been enslaved, but we are powerless, because our fields and our vineyards belong to others."

When I heard their outcry and these charges, I was very angry. I pondered them in my mind and then accused the nobles and officials. I told them, "You are charging your own people interest!" So I called together a large meeting to deal with them and said: "As far as possible, we have bought back our fellow Jews who were sold to the Gentiles. Now you are selling your own people, only for them to be sold back to us!" They kept quiet, because they could find nothing to say.

So I continued, "What you are doing is not right. Shouldn't you walk in the fear of our God to avoid the reproach of our Gentile enemies? I and my brothers and my men are also lending the people money and grain. But let us stop charging interest! Give back to them immediately their fields, vineyards, olive groves and houses, and also the interest you are charging them—one percent of the money, grain, new wine and olive oil."

"We will give it back," they said. "And we will not demand anything more from them. We will do as you say."

Then I summoned the priests and made the nobles and officials take an oath to do what they had promised. I also shook out the folds of my robe and said, "In this way may God shake out of their house and possessions anyone who does not keep this promise. So may such a person be shaken out and emptied!"

At this the whole assembly said, "Amen," and praised the Lord. And the people did as they had promised.

Moreover, from the twentieth year of King Artaxerxes, when I was appointed to be their governor in the land of Judah, until his thirty-second year—twelve years—neither I nor my brothers ate the food allotted to the governor. But the earlier governors—those preceding me—placed a heavy burden on the people and took forty shekels of silver from them in addition to food and wine. Their assistants also lorded it over the people. But out of reverence for God I did not act like that. Instead, I devoted myself to the work on this wall. All my men were assembled there for the work; we did not acquire any land.

Furthermore, a hundred and fifty Jews and officials ate at my table, as well as those who came to us from the surrounding nations. Each day one ox, six choice sheep and some poultry were prepared for me, and every ten days an abundant supply of wine of all kinds. In spite of all this, I never demanded the food allotted to the governor, because the demands were heavy on these people.

Remember me with favor, my God, for all I have done for these people.

Doing God's work causes opposition and fury, especially when Satan has had it all his own way for so long. Indeed, many of us have adopted the world's ways and are virtually part of the world in the way we operate. We do things the same way as the world, we often think the same way as the world, and we mostly look the same as the world.

This will have to change, and it has to change of a necessity. When we begin to rebuild the walls, we will face ridicule which will escalate to outright opposition. Still, the truth is that as we continue to build, the opposition and determination of the opposition to silence us and stop our work will only increase.

We already see how this world stops preaching and teaching God's word. We already see how preachers are arrested in the street for preaching God's word. I'm not talking about China, North Korea or Iran here. This is already happening in the USA, UK, and Scotland. Imagine how it will be when we get going and start rebuilding the walls.

BSLE: Have we seen any opposition in our area? Have we tried to preach in the street?

Be prepared that the world will fight us in any way they can, and we will suffer famine just the same as the Jews did at this time. In our country, so much of our resources to feed ourselves depend on the government, and when we do not conform to their ways, they will find ways to defund us and withdraw our resources.

Those who do not conform will not be eligible for any benefits, even a pension we have paid for years. They will not be eligible to work for any government agency or any company that receive funds from the government. They will not be eligible to receive certain tax breaks, so that what we do have will be taken away from us.

Do not be under any illusion that what we do will be easy. Do not kid yourselves that we live in a democracy, and these things could never happen here. Unfortunately, democracy is fast slipping away from us in this country. The government's will in this country is not to support the Church of Christianity, and we will be imprisoned, fined, and targeted in every way they can to deter us from our work.

BSLE: Do we really believe that these things could happen in our country? Do we have examples of any countries which have changed dramatically and Churches are now persecuted?

The rebuilding of the walls will come under tremendous stress and fierce opposition and will almost be unbearable for some. Nevertheless, a cry will arise from many people involved in the work, and it will be the time for all of God's people to pull together and support each other.

The Church will have to return to the position it was in during the early chapters of Acts, where no one counted what he had as his own but brought all they had to the feet of the Apostles for distribution as necessary.

If we look back on the history of our local area, we see this in practice. Looking back to fifty or one hundred years ago, some struggled, and everybody chipped in and helped out. For example, a widowed woman turned half of her house into a shop, and people around shopped there to help out.

People struggling with life and putting a meal on the table would find a food parcel left outside their door. Kids clothes would be handed down, still in good condition to those who could not afford to buy new clothes for their kids. There were numerous ways in which we all helped out the poor and needy.

BSLE: Do we have programs in place to help those in need? Do you think we will need them?

Sadly, that is gone, a thing of the past, replaced by a dependence on the central government who can withhold at their pleasure. We have all bought into this new social welfare system which does not operate so efficiently as God's system. It is full of injustices and abuse and ultimately will be a tool for those who want to hinder the work of God.

It is interesting also to note in verse 17 that some came from other nations and needed to be fed. What does that mean for us in this day?

When our revival begins, many will be affected, and a burden of repentance will come upon many without discrimination. However, when converts come from other faiths, such as Islam, they will be cast out and ostracised by their own people and will need our help.

I believe that in the next revival, with the UK now being a multi-faith community, there will be many, many from other faiths who come under conviction and turn to God.

BSLE: Are there many in your area from other faiths? How will you be able to help them when they are cast out from their own community?

Brothers and sisters, a time of famine will come for many. Be ready to respond to the need and not let this hinder the rebuilding of God's Church.

There is much talk in this passage of oppression by the officials against the ordinary people. It is my feeling that in our day, this relates to some of the large prosperity Churches who insist on their congregation putting in large donations while the Church leaders are millionaires.

This practice must be stopped, and all the Church leaders must make common cause with the congregation members. Jesus never made himself any different from the ordinary people and never lorded it over them, even though he, of all men, had the right. If Jesus humbled himself, then we must do no less.

The Church leaders need to look towards their members and examine how they can help them with the basics of life. It is a great work being carried out, and all our number must be kept in the best of spirit and body.

BSLE: Discuss the entire chapter and pray about what you have discussed. Encourage group to read next chapter before meeting again.

CHAPTER 7

Psychological Opposition

<u>Nehemiah 6</u>
When word came to Sanballat, Tobiah, Geshem the Arab and the rest of our enemies that I had rebuilt the wall and not a gap was left in it—though up to that time I had not set the doors in the gates— Sanballat and Geshem sent me this message: "Come, let us meet together in one of the villages on the plain of Ono."

But they were scheming to harm me; so I sent messengers to them with this reply: "I am carrying on a great project and cannot go down. Why should the work stop while I leave it and go down to you?" Four times they sent me the same message, and each time I gave them the same answer.

Then, the fifth time, Sanballat sent his aide to me with the same message, and in his hand was an unsealed letter in which was written:

"It is reported among the nations—and Geshem says it is true—that you and the Jews are plotting to revolt, and therefore you are building the wall. Moreover, according to these reports you are about to become their king and have even appointed prophets to make this proclamation about you in Jerusalem: 'There is a king in Judah!' Now this report will get back to the king; so come, let us meet together."

I sent him this reply: "Nothing like what you are saying is happening; you are just making it up out of your head."

They were all trying to frighten us, thinking, "Their hands will get too weak for the work, and it will not be completed."

But I prayed, "Now strengthen my hands."

One day I went to the house of Shemaiah son of Delaiah, the son of Mehetabel, who was shut in at his home. He said, "Let us meet in the house of God, inside the temple, and let us close the temple doors, because men are coming to kill you—by night they are coming to kill you."

But I said, "Should a man like me run away? Or should someone like me go into the temple to save his life? I will not go!" I realized that God had not sent him, but that he had prophesied against me because Tobiah and Sanballat had hired him. He had been hired to intimidate me so that I would commit a sin by doing this, and then they would give me a bad name to discredit me.

Remember Tobiah and Sanballat, my God, because of what they have done; remember also the prophet Noadiah and how she and the rest of the prophets have been trying to intimidate me. So the wall was completed on the twenty-fifth of Elul, in fifty-two days.

When all our enemies heard about this, all the surrounding nations were afraid and lost their self-confidence, because they realized that this work had been done with the help of our God.

Also, in those days the nobles of Judah were sending many letters to Tobiah, and replies from Tobiah kept coming to them. For many in Judah were under oath to him, since he was son-in-law to Shekaniah son of Arah, and his son Jehohanan had married the daughter of Meshullam son of Berekiah. Moreover, they kept reporting to me his good deeds and then telling him what I said. And Tobiah sent letters to intimidate me.

The work is progressing, and everything that the opposition had tried had failed. The walls have been rebuilt, and just the gates had to be put in place. The enemy finally concludes that they cannot stop this work by their standard procedures, so they start to plot ways to bring down the leaders. They know Nehemiah is the driving force behind it all, so they reason, if they can get rid of him, then everything else will fall apart.

As we complete the rebuilding of the Church's walls, open opposition will no longer be the focus, but plotting in every way will become the norm. There will be nothing they will not sanction now. There will be no depths they will not go to stop the work.

BSLE: Is our own government capable of this level of opposition to the Church?

They now realise that the walls have been repaired and only the gates need to be hung. They are into panic mode now as they realise that their ultimate access to the Church will be cut off once the gates are in place. Lack of gates have been their advantage until now, and this shows as their agents within the Church start to show their true colours.

It is amazing how everyone working so hard for the past weeks, yet when it comes to this point, so many enemy operatives crawl out into the open in a final attempt to put a stop to hanging the gates.

When we arrive at this point in the rebuilding, we will be amazed at the number of Satan's people within the Church and take their final stand for their master. Even today, our Church is entirely infiltrated by agents of the enemy who intend to keep it unchallenging, unproductive and unnoticeable within the world.

BSLE: Do we see any sign of the enemy within our own local Church?

Despite the opposition throwing everything they have at it, they will not succeed, and when the walls are completed, the opposition from the enemy will be thrown into disarray. There will be much fear among the enemy circles as they realise that God has been in this movement from the very start.

There will be much talk and much discussion among the enemy on what they should do next, but the fight will go out of them, and they will, as mentioned in verse sixteen, have lost their confidence.

This is when the Church leaders will come under tremendous pressure and be in fear for their lives. In the text, many attempts were made on Nehemiah's life, and we should not think for one moment that this cannot happen in our time. We are now at a point where the opposition is desperate and will stop at nothing, even murder.

Nothing has changed in the past few thousand years, and the opposition will attempt anything to stop the work, including murder if that is what is needed. We need to be more determined than the opposition, and we need to support and protect our leaders in any way we can.

BSLE: Do we believe that this scenario is possible? Are we ready for it?

We also need to be discerning as many false prophets and teachers will arise and try to confuse and demoralise the Church. There may well be many who we have worshipped alongside for a very long time who will try to divert us from the truth. Many who we thought belonged to the Lord will finally show their true allegiance.

The final task is to put the gates in place, and this will address the final problem of those within who do not have a place there. So we are finally approaching the end of the rebuilding and now coming to the point where revival can start.

Yes, you read that correctly. Revival has not yet started. All this must be done before revival comes. When the walls are rebuilt and the gates hung, then the world will look at the Church in a completely different light. The Church will no longer be sending out mixed messages. The Church will finally have returned to her proper place as the light and salt of the world, and the world will stand up and take notice and be drawn to it.

The building of the walls has now been completed, and although it has been very intense and wearisome, it has happened relatively quickly, only fifty-two days since they started rebuilding.

The rebuilding of the Church before revival will be similarly fast but intensive. When this is done, there will be great expectations and excitement in the Church as we all sense God's presence with us in a way we have not felt for some time, if ever.

BSLE: Discuss the entire chapter and pray about what you have discussed. Encourage group to read next chapter before meeting again.

CHAPTER 8

Taking Stock

<u>Nehemiah Chapter 7</u>
After the wall had been rebuilt and I had set the doors in place, the gatekeepers, the musicians and the Levites were appointed. I put in charge of Jerusalem my brother Hanani, along with Hananiah the commander of the citadel, because he was a man of integrity and feared God more than most people do. I said to them, "The gates of Jerusalem are not to be opened until the sun is hot. While the gatekeepers are still on duty, have them shut the doors and bar them. Also appoint residents of Jerusalem as guards, some at their posts and some near their own houses."
The List of the Exiles Who Returned
Now the city was large and spacious, but there were few people in it, and the houses had not yet been rebuilt. So my God put it into my heart to assemble the nobles, the officials and the common people for registration by families. I found the genealogical record of those who had been the first to return. This is what I found written there:
These are the people of the province who came up from the captivity of the exiles whom Nebuchadnezzar king of Babylon had taken captive (they returned to Jerusalem and Judah, each to his own town, in com-

pany with Zerubbabel, Joshua, Nehemiah, Azariah, Raamiah, Nahamani, Mordecai, Bilshan, Mispereth, Bigvai, Nehum and Baanah):

The list of the men of Israel:
the descendants of Parosh 2,172
of Shephatiah 372
of Arah 652
of Pahath-Moab (through the line of Jeshua and Joab) 2,818
of Elam 1,254
of Zattu 845
of Zakkai 760
of Binnui 648
of Bebai 628
of Azgad 2,322
of Adonikam 667
of Bigvai 2,067
of Adin 655
of Ater (through Hezekiah) 98
of Hashum 328
of Bezai 324
of Hariph 112
of Gibeon 95
the men of Bethlehem and Netophah 188
of Anathoth 128
of Beth Azmaveth 42
of Kiriath Jearim, Kephirah and Beeroth 743
of Ramah and Geba 621
of Mikmash 122
of Bethel and Ai 123
of the other Nebo 52
of the other Elam 1,254
of Harim 320

of Jericho 345
of Lod, Hadid and Ono 721
of Senaah 3,930
The priests:
the descendants of Jedaiah (through the family of Jeshua) 973
of Immer 1,052
of Pashhur 1,247
of Harim 1,017
The Levites:
the descendants of Jeshua (through Kadmiel through the line of Hodaviah) 74
The musicians:
the descendants of Asaph 148
The gatekeepers:
the descendants of
Shallum, Ater, Talmon, Akkub, Hatita and Shobai 138
The temple servants:
the descendants of
Ziha, Hasupha, Tabbaoth,
Keros, Sia, Padon,
Lebana, Hagaba, Shalmai,
Hanan, Giddel, Gahar,
Reaiah, Rezin, Nekoda,
Gazzam, Uzza, Paseah,
Besai, Meunim, Nephusim,
Bakbuk, Hakupha, Harhur,
Bazluth, Mehida, Harsha,
Barkos, Sisera, Temah,
Neziah and Hatipha
The descendants of the servants of Solomon:
the descendants of

Sotai, Sophereth, Perida,
Jaala, Darkon, Giddel,
Shephatiah, Hattil,
Pokereth-Hazzebaim and Amon

The temple servants and the descendants of the servants of Solomon 392

The following came up from the towns of Tel Melah, Tel Harsha, Kerub, Addon and Immer, but they could not show that their families were descended from Israel:

the descendants of
Delaiah, Tobiah and Nekoda 642

And from among the priests:

the descendants of

Hobaiah, Hakkoz and Barzillai (a man who had married a daughter of Barzillai the Gileadite and was called by that name).

These searched for their family records, but they could not find them and so were excluded from the priesthood as unclean. The governor, therefore, ordered them not to eat any of the most sacred food until there should be a priest ministering with the Urim and Thummim.

The whole company numbered 42,360, besides their 7,337 male and female slaves; and they also had 245 male and female singers. There were 736 horses, 245 mules, 435 camels and 6,720 donkeys.

Some of the heads of the families contributed to the work. The governor gave to the treasury 1,000 darics of gold, 50 bowls and 530 garments for priests. Some of the heads of the families gave to the treasury for the work 20,000 darics of gold and 2,200 minas of silver. The total given by the rest of the people was 20,000 darics of gold, 2,000 minas of silver and 67 garments for priests.

The priests, the Levites, the gatekeepers, the musicians and the temple servants, along with certain of the people and the rest of the Israelites, settled in their own towns.

The walls have been completed, and the gates hung. The city is secured, but there are not many people in it. Nehemiah now secures the city and appoints officials. But, very clearly by the narrative, Nehemiah still believes that the city is vulnerable to attack and must be protected.

When we eventually rebuild our walls in the Church and hang the gates, we would do well to follow this example. There is no point in building walls and putting gates in place unless we use them and monitor them to restrict entry to those who should be inside.

Satan is very wily and will try any ruse to pull down the Church, and so we must protect that which we have built and watch out for false prophets and false teachers.

After this is all done, it would seem that Nehemiah then assembled all of God's people, even those who were not active in Jerusalem. Thus, there will be a core of active people in rebuilding the Church, but there will be many more of God's people who have drifted away from the body and live their lives without any concern to God.

BSLE: Do we know many backsliders who no longer come to Church?

These backsliders should now be called back to the Church and once again restored to the Church role. However, we will most likely find many reasons why these people have not continued in the Church in the past, and we must address the problems they have faced.

These people had returned to Jerusalem under Ezra to rebuild the temple and had faced stiff opposition and trials from those ruling the land. Therefore, we cannot blame these people for failing to continue the work, which had been made all but impossible for them.

Similarly, many in our day had given up when the way became very difficult. We should not condemn them but welcome them back with open arms to a different time.

It should be noted here that the city was large and spacious but empty. We will have completed the rebuilding at this stage, but our Churches will still be largely empty. Some Christians who were backslidden will have returned, and the world will undoubtedly know about us and heard about what is going on, but we will not yet be affecting the world in a meaningful way.

BSLE: Discuss how we will feel when we get to this point.

This will be a time for arranging the people within the Church and assigning tasks. At this time, we are confident that revival is coming, and there is great excitement in the Church.

Those in the Church will be ready, willing and eager to do whatever is required to take revival to the next step, and this will be a period when the Church is getting ready. Resources will be gathered, and people put in place to minister to the new converts who are coming.

Also, officials will be appointed to continue monitoring those who come into the Church and maintain the Church's integrity. With the walls and gates now complete, it is crucial to maintain the security of the Church.

Leaders of the Church will use this time to plan for the future and assess the work's condition. It will be a time when significant resources are gathered into the Church, preparing the Church for the great harvest to come.

BSLE: Discuss the entire chapter and pray about what you have discussed. Encourage group to read next chapter before meeting again.

CHAPTER 9

Instruction

<u>Nehemiah Chapter 8</u>
When the seventh month came and the Israelites had settled in their towns, all the people came together as one in the square before the Water Gate. They told Ezra the teacher of the Law to bring out the Book of the Law of Moses, which the Lord had commanded for Israel.

So on the first day of the seventh month Ezra the priest brought the Law before the assembly, which was made up of men and women and all who were able to understand. He read it aloud from daybreak till noon as he faced the square before the Water Gate in the presence of the men, women and others who could understand. And all the people listened attentively to the Book of the Law.

Ezra, the teacher of the Law stood on a high wooden platform built for the occasion. Beside him on his right stood Mattithiah, Shema, Anaiah, Uriah, Hilkiah and Maaseiah; and on his left were Pedaiah, Mishael, Malkijah, Hashum, Hashbaddanah, Zechariah and Meshullam.

Ezra opened the book. All the people could see him because he was standing above them; and as he opened it, the people all stood up. Ezra praised the Lord, the great God; and all the people lifted their hands and responded, "Amen! Amen!" Then they bowed down and worshiped the Lord with their faces to the ground.

The Levites—Jeshua, Bani, Sherebiah, Jamin, Akkub, Shabbethai, Hodiah, Maaseiah, Kelita, Azariah, Jozabad, Hanan and Pelaiah—instructed the people in the Law while the people were standing there. They read from the Book of the Law of God, making it clear and giving the meaning so that the people understood what was being read.

Then Nehemiah the governor, Ezra the priest and teacher of the Law, and the Levites who were instructing the people said to them all, "This day is holy to the Lord your God. Do not mourn or weep." For all the people had been weeping as they listened to the words of the Law.

Nehemiah said, "Go and enjoy choice food and sweet drinks, and send some to those who have nothing prepared. This day is holy to our Lord. Do not grieve, for the joy of the Lord is your strength."

The Levites calmed all the people, saying, "Be still, for this is a holy day. Do not grieve."

Then all the people went away to eat and drink, to send portions of food and to celebrate with great joy, because they now understood the words that had been made known to them.

On the second day of the month, the heads of all the families, along with the priests and the Levites, gathered around Ezra the teacher to give attention to the words of the Law. They found written in the Law, which the Lord had commanded through Moses, that the Israelites were to live in temporary shelters during the festival of the seventh month and that they should proclaim this word and spread it throughout their towns and in Jerusalem: "Go out into the hill country and bring back branches from olive and wild olive trees, and from myrtles, palms and shade trees, to make temporary shelters"—as it is written.

So the people went out and brought back branches and built themselves temporary shelters on their own roofs, in their courtyards, in the courts of the house of God and in the square by the Water Gate and the one by the Gate of Ephraim. The whole company that had returned from exile built temporary shelters and lived in them. From the days of Joshua son of Nun until that day, the Israelites had not celebrated it like this. And their joy was very great.

Day after day, from the first day to the last, Ezra read from the Book of the Law of God. They celebrated the festival for seven days, and on the eighth day, in accordance with the regulation, there was an assembly.

When all of God's people are assembled, it is time for the instruction to begin. For the first time, perhaps, in a long time, some of the people are hearing the word of God. They do not listen to opinions from a pastor or a teacher, but the direct word of God read and expounded to them.

Whenever Ezra stands to read the word, the entire congregation stands, and we can see that there is a profound respect for the word. But, once they hear the word, there is also grief because they suddenly realise how far away from God's precepts they had wandered.

BSLE: How much respect is there for God's word in these days? Within the world, but also within the Church.

Ezra read the word from early morning to midday, and the result was weeping among the people when they heard the true word of God. Ezra blessed the people, and the people worshipped God, which marked a change in the City's status. No longer were they mourning and grieving, but they were to rejoice and celebrate.

When all of God's people assemble in Church, a great instruction will begin. At first, there will be tears as past sins and failures are remembered, but this will quickly change to celebration once all recognize that a true revival is underway, underpinned by the repentance of God's people.

A healthy respect for the word of God will return, and the people of God will commence worship like hasn't been heard in a very long time.

This will also represent a massive turning point for the Church, and it will now move into full revival mode with grand celebrations and praising of God.

BSLE: Can any of the gathered group remember a time when there was great celebration and joy?

Notably, the people gathered as one. The people were in unity, and this was probably the first time these people had ever been united since their birth. The word enthrals all the people, and not one person will go away until dismissed. A great time of worship will begin as the people realise what God has done for them and how faithful he has been to them.

The mourning and weeping at how far they have fallen will change to rejoicing as the Lord commands blessing upon the people. Then, finally, a great feast and festival will commence, and the people will worship the Lord in unity.

Just like these inhabitants of Jerusalem, old truth and customs will be unearthed from the study of God's word, and all the people will be eager to live Godly lives and celebrate and glorify God. There will be much reading of God's word, and all the assembly shall be intent on hearing the word.

BSLE: Discuss the entire chapter and pray about what you have discussed. Encourage group to read next chapter before meeting again.

CHAPTER 10

Confession

<u>Nehemiah Chapter 9</u>

On the twenty-fourth day of the same month, the Israelites gathered together, fasting and wearing sackcloth and putting dust on their heads. Those of Israelite descent had separated themselves from all foreigners. They stood in their places and confessed their sins and the sins of their ancestors. They stood where they were and read from the Book of the Law of the Lord their God for a quarter of the day, and spent another quarter in confession and in worshiping the Lord their God. Standing on the stairs of the Levites were Jeshua, Bani, Kadmiel, Shebaniah, Bunni, Sherebiah, Bani and Kenani. They cried out with loud voices to the Lord their God. And the Levites—Jeshua, Kadmiel, Bani, Hashabneiah, Sherebiah, Hodiah, Shebaniah and Pethahiah—said: "Stand up and praise the Lord your God, who is from everlasting to everlasting."

"Blessed be your glorious name, and may it be exalted above all blessing and praise. You alone are the Lord. You made the heavens, even the highest heavens, and all their starry host, the earth and all that is on it, the seas and all that is in them. You give life to everything, and the multitudes of heaven worship you.

"You are the Lord God, who chose Abram and brought him out of Ur of the Chaldeans and named him Abraham. You found his heart faithful to you, and you made a covenant with him to give to his descendants the land of the Canaanites, Hittites, Amorites, Perizzites, Jebusites and Girgashites. You have kept your promise because you are righteous.

"You saw the suffering of our ancestors in Egypt; you heard their cry at the Red Sea. You sent signs and wonders against Pharaoh, against all his officials and all the people of his land, for you knew how arrogantly the Egyptians treated them. You made a name for yourself, which remains to this day. You divided the sea before them, so that they passed through it on dry ground, but you hurled their pursuers into the depths, like a stone into mighty waters. By day you led them with a pillar of cloud, and by night with a pillar of fire to give them light on the way they were to take.

"You came down on Mount Sinai; you spoke to them from heaven. You gave them regulations and laws that are just and right, and decrees and commands that are good. You made known to them your holy Sabbath and gave them commands, decrees and laws through your servant Moses. In their hunger you gave them bread from heaven and in their thirst you brought them water from the rock; you told them to go in and take possession of the land you had sworn with uplifted hand to give them.

"But they, our ancestors, became arrogant and stiff-necked, and they did not obey your commands. They refused to listen and failed to remember the miracles you performed among them. They became stiff-necked and in their rebellion appointed a leader in order to return to their slavery. But you are a forgiving God, gracious and compassionate, slow to anger and abounding in love. Therefore you did not desert them, even when they cast for themselves an image of a calf and said, 'This is your god, who brought you up out of Egypt,' or when they committed awful blasphemies.

"Because of your great compassion you did not abandon them in the wilderness. By day the pillar of cloud did not fail to guide them on their path, nor the pillar of fire by night to shine on the way they were to take. You gave your good Spirit to instruct them. You did not withhold your manna from their mouths, and you gave them water for their thirst. For forty years you sustained them in the wilderness; they lacked nothing, their clothes did not wear out nor did their feet become swollen.

"You gave them kingdoms and nations, allotting to them even the remotest frontiers. They took over the country of Sihon king of Heshbon and the country of Og king of Bashan. You made their children as numerous as the stars in the sky, and you brought them into the land that you told their parents to enter and possess. Their children went in and took possession of the land. You subdued before them the Canaanites, who lived in the land; you gave the Canaanites into their hands, along with their kings and the peoples of the land, to deal with them as they pleased. They captured fortified cities and fertile land; they took possession of houses filled with all kinds of good things, wells already dug, vineyards, olive groves and fruit trees in abundance. They ate to the full and were well-nourished; they reveled in your great goodness.

"But they were disobedient and rebelled against you; they turned their backs on your law. They killed your prophets, who had warned them in order to turn them back to you; they committed awful blasphemies. So you delivered them into the hands of their enemies, who oppressed them. But when they were oppressed they cried out to you. From heaven you heard them, and in your great compassion you gave them deliverers, who rescued them from the hand of their enemies.

"But as soon as they were at rest, they again did what was evil in your sight. Then you abandoned them to the hand of their enemies so that they ruled over them. And when they cried out to you again, you heard from heaven, and in your compassion you delivered them time after time.

"You warned them in order to turn them back to your law, but they became arrogant and disobeyed your commands. They sinned against your ordinances, of which you said, 'The person who obeys them will live by them.' Stubbornly they turned their backs on you, became stiff-necked and refused to listen. For many years you were patient with them. By your Spirit you warned them through your prophets. Yet they paid no attention, so you gave them into the hands of the neighboring peoples. But in your great mercy you did not put an end to them or abandon them, for you are a gracious and merciful God.

"Now therefore, our God, the great God, mighty and awesome, who keeps his covenant of love, do not let all this hardship seem trifling in your eyes—the hardship that has come on us, on our kings and leaders, on our priests and prophets, on our ancestors and all your people, from the days of the kings of Assyria until today. In all that has happened to us, you have remained righteous; you have acted faithfully, while we acted wickedly. Our kings, our leaders, our priests and our ancestors did not follow your law; they did not pay attention to your commands or the statutes you warned them to keep. Even while they were in their kingdom, enjoying your great goodness to them in the spacious and fertile land you gave them, they did not serve you or turn from their evil ways.

"But see, we are slaves today, slaves in the land you gave our ancestors so they could eat its fruit and the other good things it produces. Because of our sins, its abundant harvest goes to the kings you have placed over us. They rule over our bodies and our cattle as they please. We are in great distress.

The Agreement of the People

"In view of all this, we are making a binding agreement, putting it in writing, and our leaders, our Levites and our priests are affixing their seals to it."

When we read this summary of the history of the Israelis from the time they left Egypt until the time when they were carried away into captivity, it is striking to read a parallel narrative to the church over the past two thousand years.

The Church has been the same as the Children of Israel because they have continually failed and tested God, yet God has remained faithful to the Church. The continual falling away and restoration could be talking about the Church, as we can trace a similar pattern in the Church's history.

BSLE: Discuss the history of the Church in your area.

Truly nothing is new under the sun, and the Old Testament, when we study it, provides us with much enlightenment and examples to follow. There is no better example for us to follow than the example we now see unfolding before us.

The people, as one, repent and confess not only their own sins but also the sins of their fathers. They catalogue how time after time, their forefathers had rebelled against God and yet how wonderfully and mercifully God had dealt with them, and only after many failures had let them be taken into captivity.

They finish up their confession by concluding that they too had acted wickedly, but God had been just and righteous and then signed an agreement to return to God faithfully.

BSLE: If you feel it necessary, hold a time of prayer and confession.

After many revivals in the Church, similar things have happened. Usually, a new denomination appears who is rigorous in defending the faith and pledge allegiance to God and his word. It is expected that something similar will happen at the next revival, although it will not necessarily be a new denomination.

For sure, like the Israelis, it will only be a remnant that will go forward to begin rebuilding the Church. This small remnant will also remember and recall the Church's history and how their forefathers have failed God just like the Israelis had. They will marvel that God still has patience and compassion for them.

The entire experience will deeply touch those in the Church who will once again intend to follow God to their utmost. However, it would be folly for us to think it will be different this time. Human nature means we are very fickle and stubborn. This pattern of falling away has been the same now for four thousand years, and we should simply enjoy our time of refreshing and try our best to leave a legacy to go forward.

Although our Churches are in a terrible state right now, past generations have left us a great legacy to build on. We are not building from scratch. Although the walls are broken down, the stones are still there. We must do all in our power to leave a similar legacy for future generations.

BSLE: Discuss the entire chapter and pray about what you have discussed. Encourage group to read next chapter before meeting again.

CHAPTER 11

Rededication

Nehemiah Chapter 10
Those who sealed it were:
Nehemiah the governor, the son of Hacaliah.
Zedekiah, Seraiah, Azariah, Jeremiah,
Pashhur, Amariah, Malkijah,
Hattush, Shebaniah, Malluk,
Harim, Meremoth, Obadiah,
Daniel, Ginnethon, Baruch,
Meshullam, Abijah, Mijamin,
Maaziah, Bilgai and Shemaiah.
These were the priests.
The Levites:
Jeshua son of Azaniah, Binnui of the sons of Henadad, Kadmiel,
and their associates: Shebaniah,
Hodiah, Kelita, Pelaiah, Hanan,
Mika, Rehob, Hashabiah,
Zakkur, Sherebiah, Shebaniah,
Hodiah, Bani and Beninu.

The leaders of the people:
Parosh, Pahath-Moab, Elam, Zattu, Bani,
Bunni, Azgad, Bebai,
Adonijah, Bigvai, Adin,
Ater, Hezekiah, Azzur,
Hodiah, Hashum, Bezai,
Hariph, Anathoth, Nebai,
Magpiash, Meshullam, Hezir,
Meshezabel, Zadok, Jaddua,
Pelatiah, Hanan, Anaiah,
Hoshea, Hananiah, Hasshub,
Hallohesh, Pilha, Shobek,
Rehum, Hashabnah, Maaseiah,
Ahiah, Hanan, Anan,
Malluk, Harim and Baanah.

"The rest of the people—priests, Levites, gatekeepers, musicians, temple servants and all who separated themselves from the neighboring peoples for the sake of the Law of God, together with their wives and all their sons and daughters who are able to understand— all these now join their fellow Israelites the nobles, and bind themselves with a curse and an oath to follow the Law of God given through Moses the servant of God and to obey carefully all the commands, regulations and decrees of the Lord our Lord.

"We promise not to give our daughters in marriage to the peoples around us or take their daughters for our sons.

"When the neighboring peoples bring merchandise or grain to sell on the Sabbath, we will not buy from them on the Sabbath or on any holy day. Every seventh year we will forgo working the land and will cancel all debts.

"We assume the responsibility for carrying out the commands to give a third of a shekel each year for the service of the house of our God: for the bread set out on the table; for the regular grain offerings and burnt offerings; for the offerings on the Sabbaths, at the New Moon feasts and at the appointed festivals; for the holy offerings; for sin offerings to make atonement for Israel; and for all the duties of the house of our God.

"We—the priests, the Levites and the people—have cast lots to determine when each of our families is to bring to the house of our God at set times each year a contribution of wood to burn on the altar of the Lord our God, as it is written in the Law.

"We also assume responsibility for bringing to the house of the Lord each year the first fruits of our crops and of every fruit tree.

"As it is also written in the Law, we will bring the firstborn of our sons and of our cattle, of our herds and of our flocks to the house of our God, to the priests ministering there.

"Moreover, we will bring to the storerooms of the house of our God, to the priests, the first of our ground meal, of our grain offerings, of the fruit of all our trees and of our new wine and olive oil. And we will bring a tithe of our crops to the Levites, for it is the Levites who collect the tithes in all the towns where we work. A priest descended from Aaron is to accompany the Levites when they receive the tithes, and the Levites are to bring a tenth of the tithes up to the house of our God, to the storerooms of the treasury. The people of Israel, including the Levites, are to bring their contributions of grain, new wine and olive oil to the storerooms, where the articles for the sanctuary and for the ministering priests, the gatekeepers and the musicians are also kept.

"We will not neglect the house of our God."

The people make a formal declaration to follow God and return to a very rigid interpretation of the law. The Church, which has moved away from the law of God for years, will immediately pledge to return to a strict understanding of the law and will require all God's people to uphold it.

As this unfolds, we will see a reversal in the direction in which society as a whole is travelling. Where society has moved towards an 'anything goes' Sunday, this will reverse as there will be so many people who can no longer attend events and so many people who refuse to shop or work on a Sunday.

We will see a return of school assemblies that honour God and prayers to the classroom. We will see a return of Parliament to a place where our laws are modelled on the laws of God.

Companies and sports clubs will all clamour to live up to the law of God, and sport and work on a Sunday will once again be only for essential workers.

BSLE: Are these things we are currently praying for? Are we ready to start leading the nation again?

Once again, the Church will start leading the nation, rather than the nation leading the Church. This will, in turn, begin a season of prosperity for our country.

In the Church, the love of God will work its way into every area of our lives. Where in the past, we got on with our lives and fitted Church around it, we will now fit our lives around the Church and God's will.

Young people will begin to consult God about who they should take for a life partner, and a younger generation will emerge who will begin to drive the revival. The younger generation will be eager to sit and listen to the older generation pass on their knowledge of the scriptures. Bible studies and prayer meetings will be a daily event.

The emerging generation who reverence God will influence politicians who are always eager to follow votes. Still, voters who are now seeing clearer than they have done for some time will have no time for politicians who only seek votes and are manifestly against the Church. As a result, a new breed of politicians will begin to emerge who will change our government and our country.

A new generation of believers will also revolutionise the educational system and restore common sense and common decency to our classrooms and lecture halls.

Prisons will not escape the change, and many will begin to empty, and the prisons themselves will become a centre of revival as God's love reaches into men and women who have little hope in this world and give them real hope for the first time in their lives. Many will undergo a complete transformation.

Such a transformation in the Church and its people will bring all their resources into the Church to build it up and glorify God. There will no longer be a shortage of elders and deacons in the Church. The people will count it as an honour to serve, and the only thing holding many back will be the feeling that they are not worthy.

BSLE: Discuss the entire chapter and pray about what you have discussed. Encourage group to read next chapter before meeting again.

CHAPTER 12

Restoration

Nehemiah Chapter 11
Now the leaders of the people settled in Jerusalem. The rest of the people cast lots to bring one out of every ten of them to live in Jerusalem, the holy city, while the remaining nine were to stay in their own towns. The people commended all who volunteered to live in Jerusalem.

These are the provincial leaders who settled in Jerusalem (now some Israelites, priests, Levites, temple servants and descendants of Solomon's servants lived in the towns of Judah, each on their own property in the various towns, while other people from both Judah and Benjamin lived in Jerusalem):

From the descendants of Judah:

Athaiah son of Uzziah, the son of Zechariah, the son of Amariah, the son of Shephatiah, the son of Mahalalel, a descendant of Perez; and Maaseiah son of Baruch, the son of Kol-Hozeh, the son of Hazaiah, the son of Adaiah, the son of Joiarib, the son of Zechariah, a descendant of Shelah. The descendants of Perez who lived in Jerusalem totaled 468 men of standing.

From the descendants of Benjamin:

Sallu son of Meshullam, the son of Joed, the son of Pedaiah, the son of Kolaiah, the son of Maaseiah, the son of Ithiel, the son of Jeshaiah, and his followers, Gabbai and Sallai—928 men. Joel son of Zikri was their chief officer, and Judah son of Hassenuah was over the New Quarter of the city.

From the priests:

Jedaiah; the son of Joiarib; Jakin; Seraiah son of Hilkiah, the son of Meshullam, the son of Zadok, the son of Meraioth, the son of Ahitub, the official in charge of the house of God, and their associates, who carried on work for the temple—822 men; Adaiah son of Jeroham, the son of Pelaliah, the son of Amzi, the son of Zechariah, the son of Pashhur, the son of Malkijah, and his associates, who were heads of families—242 men; Amashsai son of Azarel, the son of Ahzai, the son of Meshillemoth, the son of Immer, and his associates, who were men of standing—128. Their chief officer was Zabdiel son of Haggedolim.

From the Levites:

Shemaiah son of Hasshub, the son of Azrikam, the son of Hashabiah, the son of Bunni; Shabbethai and Jozabad, two of the heads of the Levites, who had charge of the outside work of the house of God; Mattaniah son of Mika, the son of Zabdi, the son of Asaph, the director who led in thanksgiving and prayer; Bakbukiah, second among his associates; and Abda son of Shammua, the son of Galal, the son of Jeduthun. The Levites in the holy city totaled 284.

The gatekeepers:

Akkub, Talmon and their associates, who kept watch at the gates—172 men.

The rest of the Israelites, with the priests and Levites, were in all the towns of Judah, each on their ancestral property.

The temple servants lived on the hill of Ophel, and Ziha and Gishpa were in charge of them.

The chief officer of the Levites in Jerusalem was Uzzi son of Bani, the son of Hashabiah, the son of Mattaniah, the son of Mika. Uzzi was one of Asaph's descendants, who were the musicians responsible for the service of the house of God. The musicians were under the king's orders, which regulated their daily activity.

Pethahiah son of Meshezabel, one of the descendants of Zerah son of Judah, was the king's agent in all affairs relating to the people.

As for the villages with their fields, some of the people of Judah lived in Kiriath Arba and its surrounding settlements, in Dibon and its settlements, in Jekabzeel and its villages, in Jeshua, in Moladah, in Beth Pelet, in Hazar Shual, in Beersheba and its settlements, in Ziklag, in Mekonah and its settlements, in En Rimmon, in Zorah, in Jarmuth, Zanoah, Adullam and their villages, in Lachish and its fields, and in Azekah and its settlements. So they were living all the way from Beersheba to the Valley of Hinnom.

The descendants of the Benjamites from Geba lived in Mikmash, Aija, Bethel and its settlements, in Anathoth, Nob and Ananiah, in Hazor, Ramah and Gittaim, in Hadid, Zeboim and Neballat, in Lod and Ono, and in Ge Harashim.

Some of the divisions of the Levites of Judah settled in Benjamin.

The Church will become very practical once it has been rededicated and set on a new path. There will be a concern for all aspects of the people, and many will volunteer to help out in every way the people need.

There will be a considerable increase in those going forward for full-time work in the Kingdom of God. Bible colleges will be packed full. Every member of the Church will be more than willing to support those willing to work full time in the Church.

There will be huge respect for those who work full-time in the gospel work, and fathers and mothers will once again be proud for their children to go into the ministry. Once again, our country will become a sender of missionaries to other parts of the world.

BSLE: How many missionaries have been sent out from your Church in recent years? Are there any here felt led to be leaders?

For the first time in many years, people will again begin to refer to our country as a Christian country, and our nation will again start to take on a revered position internationally.

In every walk of life, Christians will begin to control and dominate the agenda and path society is following. Schools, colleges and all manner of new projects will take on the name of Jesus and be formed with Biblical standards and basis.

We will enter a period where Christianity is taking the lead. There will be new songwriters, poets, musicians, preachers, teachers, leaders, politicians and many more professional people who will rise to worldwide fame and achieve such status that they will be remembered for generations to come.

If we look back in history, great people come out of revivals, such as DL Moody, The Wesleys, Fanny Crosby, Ira Sankey, John Newton, Wilberforce; the list could go on. This will be such a time, and these emerging young stars of the Church will do great things for the Lord through lives wholly given over to God.

You will note that I said young stars. I believe these will be new converts who emerge from the first throws of the revival and have their entire lives ahead of them to do great things. Our older generation will stand behind them and facilitate them in any way we can.

BSLE: Discuss the entire chapter and pray about what you have discussed. Encourage group to read next chapter before meeting again.

CHAPTER 13

Dedication

Nehemiah Chapter 12
These were the priests and Levites who returned with Zerubbabel son of Shealtiel and with Joshua:
Seraiah, Jeremiah, Ezra,
Amariah, Malluk, Hattush,
Shekaniah, Rehum, Meremoth,
Iddo, Ginnethon, Abijah,
Mijamin, Moadiah, Bilgah,
Shemaiah, Joiarib, Jedaiah,
Sallu, Amok, Hilkiah and Jedaiah.
These were the leaders of the priests and their associates in the days of Joshua.
The Levites were Jeshua, Binnui, Kadmiel, Sherebiah, Judah, and also Mattaniah, who, together with his associates, was in charge of the songs of thanksgiving. Bakbukiah and Unni, their associates, stood opposite them in the services.

Joshua was the father of Joiakim, Joiakim the father of Eliashib, Eliashib the father of Joiada, Joiada the father of Jonathan, and Jonathan the father of Jaddua.

In the days of Joiakim, these were the heads of the priestly families:
of Seraiah's family, Meraiah;
of Jeremiah's, Hananiah;
of Ezra's, Meshullam;
of Amariah's, Jehohanan;
of Malluk's, Jonathan;
of Shekaniah's, Joseph;
of Harim's, Adna;
of Meremoth's, Helkai;
of Iddo's, Zechariah;
of Ginnethon's, Meshullam;
of Abijah's, Zikri;
of Miniamin's and of Moadiah's, Piltai;
of Bilgah's, Shammua;
of Shemaiah's, Jehonathan;
of Joiarib's, Mattenai;
of Jedaiah's, Uzzi;
of Sallu's, Kallai;
of Amok's, Eber;
of Hilkiah's, Hashabiah;
of Jedaiah's, Nethanel.

The family heads of the Levites in the days of Eliashib, Joiada, Johanan and Jaddua, as well as those of the priests, were recorded in the reign of Darius the Persian. The family heads among the descendants of Levi up to the time of Johanan son of Eliashib were recorded in the book of the annals. And the leaders of the Levites were Hashabiah, Sherebiah, Jeshua son of Kadmiel, and their associates, who stood opposite them to give praise and thanksgiving, one section responding to the other, as prescribed by David the man of God.

Mattaniah, Bakbukiah, Obadiah, Meshullam, Talmon and Akkub were gatekeepers who guarded the storerooms at the gates. They served in the days of Joiakim son of Joshua, the son of Jozadak, and in the days of Nehemiah the governor and of Ezra the priest, the teacher of the Law.

At the dedication of the wall of Jerusalem, the Levites were sought out from where they lived and were brought to Jerusalem to celebrate joyfully the dedication with songs of thanksgiving and with the music of cymbals, harps and lyres. The musicians also were brought together from the region around Jerusalem—from the villages of the Netophathites, from Beth Gilgal, and from the area of Geba and Azmaveth, for the musicians had built villages for themselves around Jerusalem. When the priests and Levites had purified themselves ceremonially, they purified the people, the gates and the wall.

I had the leaders of Judah go up on top of the wall. I also assigned two large choirs to give thanks. One was to proceed on top of the wall to the right, toward the Dung Gate. Hoshaiah and half the leaders of Judah followed them, along with Azariah, Ezra, Meshullam, Judah, Benjamin, Shemaiah, Jeremiah, as well as some priests with trumpets, and also Zechariah son of Jonathan, the son of Shemaiah, the son of Mattaniah, the son of Micaiah, the son of Zakkur, the son of Asaph, and his associates—Shemaiah, Azarel, Milalai, Gilalai, Maai, Nethanel, Judah and Hanani—with musical instruments prescribed by David the man of God. Ezra the teacher of the Law led the procession. At the Fountain Gate they continued directly up the steps of the City of David on the ascent to the wall and passed above the site of David's palace to the Water Gate on the east.

The second choir proceeded in the opposite direction. I followed them on top of the wall, together with half the people—past the Tower of the Ovens to the Broad Wall, over the Gate of Ephraim, the Jeshanah

Gate, the Fish Gate, the Tower of Hananel and the Tower of the Hundred, as far as the Sheep Gate. At the Gate of the Guard they stopped.

The two choirs that gave thanks then took their places in the house of God; so did I, together with half the officials, as well as the priests—Eliakim, Maaseiah, Miniamin, Micaiah, Elioenai, Zechariah and Hananiah with their trumpets— and also Maaseiah, Shemaiah, Eleazar, Uzzi, Jehohanan, Malkijah, Elam and Ezer. The choirs sang under the direction of Jezrahiah. And on that day they offered great sacrifices, rejoicing because God had given them great joy. The women and children also rejoiced. The sound of rejoicing in Jerusalem could be heard far away.

At that time men were appointed to be in charge of the storerooms for the contributions, firstfruits and tithes. From the fields around the towns they were to bring into the storerooms the portions required by the Law for the priests and the Levites, for Judah was pleased with the ministering priests and Levites. They performed the service of their God and the service of purification, as did also the musicians and gatekeepers, according to the commands of David and his son Solomon. For long ago, in the days of David and Asaph, there had been directors for the musicians and for the songs of praise and thanksgiving to God. So in the days of Zerubbabel and of Nehemiah, all Israel contributed the daily portions for the musicians and the gatekeepers. They also set aside the portion for the other Levites, and the Levites set aside the portion for the descendants of Aaron.

Verse 43 tells us that the joy of Jerusalem was heard from afar. So shall it be at the peak of revival. All around shall know about it and will be astonished. Unbelievers around us will be drawn to the joy we exude, just to see what it is we have.

Once again we will have arrived at the answer to our prayers. How often have we prayed to see people flocking to God's house again? It will now be happening, and there will be real problems in many Churches that simply cannot house the numbers.

Smaller Churches and Churches that have remodelled with less seating will hold multiple services to cope with the number of people flocking to services every week. They will also have to begin multiple mid-week services for new converts who are hungry for the word of God.

BSLE: How would our Church cope with hundreds of people wanting to get to Church on Sunday?

Prayer meetings will be jammed packed and possibly last for hours as it is tough to get an opportunity to voice your prayer. The people will gladly bring in their tithes and offerings to support the work of the Church.

This will mark the peak of the revival, and it will be talked about around the entire world for generations to come. Excitement will abound in every town and city in the land, and when you walk down the street, the talk will not be about football or the weather but God.

People meeting each other in the street will excitedly talk about passages they have discovered in the Bible, the latest series of meetings being held, the latest converts who have been miraculously saved and the difficulty getting a seat in Church.

The joy on believers faces will be evident, and no longer will believers go around with sad looks. Instead, smiles will be the order of the day and everyone connected to the Church will be rejoicing and living life to the full.

This is the revival at its peak, and there will be a natural feeling that this is the Church as it should be. There will be a deep reverence for all things of God, and a holy fear will be present in all. Once again, there will be a buzz at Church, and when we go there, we will go expectantly, looking and expecting God to be present and for great things to happen.

BSLE: Discuss how we would feel at this point.

Baptisms and even mass baptisms will be commonplace, and the Church will hold many celebrations. Another typical celebration will be the dedication and sending out of missionaries from your Church.

Where we have come together in our Churches, held our services and then gone our own ways for the remainder of the week, the Church will now become fully integrated and have daily contact and close relations with our brothers and sisters. The Church will once again become a real functioning family.

BSLE: Discuss the entire chapter and pray about what you have discussed. Encourage group to read next chapter before meeting again.

CHAPTER 14

Reform

<u>Nehemiah Chapter 13</u>
On that day the Book of Moses was read aloud in the hearing of the people and there it was found written that no Ammonite or Moabite should ever be admitted into the assembly of God, because they had not met the Israelites with food and water but had hired Balaam to call a curse down on them. (Our God, however, turned the curse into a blessing.) When the people heard this law, they excluded from Israel all who were of foreign descent.

Before this, Eliashib the priest had been put in charge of the storerooms of the house of our God. He was closely associated with Tobiah, and he had provided him with a large room formerly used to store the grain offerings and incense and temple articles, and also the tithes of grain, new wine and olive oil prescribed for the Levites, musicians and gatekeepers, as well as the contributions for the priests.

But while all this was going on, I was not in Jerusalem, for in the thirty-second year of Artaxerxes king of Babylon, I had returned to the king. Some time later I asked his permission and came back to Jerusalem. Here I learned about the evil thing Eliashib had done in providing Tobiah a room in the courts of the house of God. I was greatly displeased and threw all Tobiah's household goods out of the room. I gave orders to purify the rooms, and then I put back into them the equipment of the house of God, with the grain offerings and the incense.

I also learned that the portions assigned to the Levites had not been given to them, and that all the Levites and musicians responsible for the service had gone back to their own fields. So I rebuked the officials and asked them, "Why is the house of God neglected?" Then I called them together and stationed them at their posts.

All Judah brought the tithes of grain, new wine and olive oil into the storerooms. I put Shelemiah the priest, Zadok the scribe, and a Levite named Pedaiah in charge of the storerooms and made Hanan son of Zakkur, the son of Mattaniah, their assistant, because they were considered trustworthy. They were made responsible for distributing the supplies to their fellow Levites.

Remember me for this, my God, and do not blot out what I have so faithfully done for the house of my God and its services.

In those days I saw people in Judah treading winepresses on the Sabbath and bringing in grain and loading it on donkeys, together with wine, grapes, figs and all other kinds of loads. And they were bringing all this into Jerusalem on the Sabbath. Therefore I warned them against selling food on that day. People from Tyre who lived in Jerusalem were bringing in fish and all kinds of merchandise and selling them in Jerusalem on the Sabbath to the people of Judah. I rebuked the nobles of Judah and said to them, "What is this wicked thing you are doing—desecrating the Sabbath day? Didn't your ancestors do the same things, so that our God brought all this calamity on us and on this city? Now you are stirring up more wrath against Israel by desecrating the Sabbath."

When evening shadows fell on the gates of Jerusalem before the Sabbath, I ordered the doors to be shut and not opened until the Sabbath was over. I stationed some of my own men at the gates so that no load could be brought in on the Sabbath day. Once or twice the merchants and sellers of all kinds of goods spent the night outside Jerusalem. But I warned them and said, "Why do you spend the night by the wall? If you do this again, I will arrest you." From that time on they no longer came on the Sabbath. Then I commanded the Levites to purify themselves and go and guard the gates in order to keep the Sabbath day holy.

Remember me for this also, my God, and show mercy to me according to your great love.

Moreover, in those days I saw men of Judah who had married women from Ashdod, Ammon and Moab. Half of their children spoke the language of Ashdod or the language of one of the other peoples, and did not know how to speak the language of Judah. I rebuked them and called curses down on them. I beat some of the men and pulled out their hair. I made them take an oath in God's name and said: "You are not to give your daughters in marriage to their sons, nor are you to take their daughters in marriage for your sons or for yourselves. Was it not because of marriages like these that Solomon king of Israel sinned? Among the many nations there was no king like him. He was loved by his God, and God made him king over all Israel, but even he was led into sin by foreign women. Must we hear now that you too are doing all this terrible wickedness and are being unfaithful to our God by marrying foreign women?"

One of the sons of Joiada son of Eliashib the high priest was son-in-law to Sanballat the Horonite. And I drove him away from me.

Remember them, my God, because they defiled the priestly office and the covenant of the priesthood and of the Levites.

So I purified the priests and the Levites of everything foreign, and assigned them duties, each to his own task. I also made provision for contributions of wood at designated times, and for the firstfruits.

Remember me with favor, my God.

Nehemiah had left Jerusalem after twelve years of revival for a period, and when he returns, already the standards have slipped to a degree we would hardly believe. After all they have seen and heard, how could they compromise in this way so quickly?

Yet, we are no different in the Church. How many great reformations and revivals have we had? How has our country been so blessed by God that it is evident that we are being rewarded for our faithfulness? How many times has God sent warnings to us and yet we turn away from him.

BSLE: How faithful are we after the way God has blessed us? How far has our Church fallen?

At one point, we are praising and worshipping God so that the whole world hears about it, and in a few short years, we have begun compromising and once again consorting with the world.

The nation takes its lead from the Church. If we consider history closely, we will see that the greatness of our country is linked to the status of our Church's faithfulness. You will find a very closely correlated link between the Church and the nation, with the nation's fortunes following the fortunes of the Church, with a lag to the timetable

What the nations do is irrelevant. What politicians do is irrelevant. The key to a nation's prosperity is in God and with God's people. When God's people begin to compromise, soon after, the country will start to decline.

If we find our nation in a terrible state, it is the Church's fault. We are the light of the world and the salt of the earth. If we are not shining a light, do not be surprised that the world is in darkness. If our salt has lost its taste, then so will the world around us.

On us, the Church, rests the fate of our nation. Not on our Queen or President. Not on politicians. The Church and her faithfulness will define the prosperity of our country. Examine the history and see if it is not so.

BSLE: What does history in the Bible and otherwise teach us about our faithfulness?

Further compromise is a given, but it is our duty, as far as possible, to stop this from happening by rigorously enforcing the standards we have set in place.

Particular importance will be on the leaders of the Church and how they rule and enforce the standards. We have seen many times in the scriptures and more recent history how refreshing lasts only until the current leadership remains. When a younger generation takes over leadership, they have never experienced a time when the Church was in ruins and have no dread of this to emphasize the importance of maintaining standards.

So we enter another long period of decline. We are now at the bottom of the slope, looking back up the hill, and we can see what has happened. At this point, the Church will be on a mountain top and unable to perceive a downward slope ahead of them.

The decline will take a long time, and the Church will remain vibrant for many years, but each subsequent generation will give up a little more until eventually those few faithful people who remain are once again pleading with God for revival.

BSLE: Discuss the entire chapter and pray about what you have discussed. If there is time, go on to read the conclusion, but also consider allocating another week to this discussion.

CHAPTER 15

Conclusion

We cannot determine what others around us do, but we can significantly influence and shape their actions by our passion and drive for revival. This story has shown how one man can achieve great things for God by dedication and refusing to compromise.

Be that man!

-
-

Neither can we determine what future generations do and how they compromise the standards of the Church. Therefore, let us resolve to uphold the Church's standards and allow no compromise of the slightest margin once the Church has been restored.

Please note, I did not say 'if' the Church is restored. Revival is coming, and only the timing is in God's hands. We still await our Nehemiah.

Be that man!

Author's Note

This marks the end of the book. If you have enjoyed this book, we would ask you to help us.

1. We would be grateful if you could leave a review of the book on Amazon. These reviews are the lifeblood of my business, and without them, I would have no new customers, and I could no longer write books.
2. I would welcome you to contact us through my author website at www.jamesgwhitelaw.com. I can assure you I am a real person and do not use a pen name. I will answer any questions you have as soon as I am able.
3. Finally, let your friends know that you read my book and enjoyed it on your social media pages.

Thank you for reading the book.

Scripture quotations taken from The Holy Bible, New International Version® NIV®

Copyright © 1973 1978 1984 2011 by Biblica, Inc.™

Used by permission. All rights reserved worldwide.

www.ingramcontent.com/pod-product-compliance
Lightning Source LLC
Chambersburg PA
CBHW021448080526
44588CB00009B/752